Why Should I Care About Steve Jobs?

A BIOGRAPHY OF STEVE JOBS JUST FOR KIDS!

Sara Smith

KidLit-O Books

ANAHEIM, CALIFORNIA

Contents

About KidLit-o

KidLit-o was started for one simple reason: our kids. They wanted to find a way to introduce classic literature to their children.

Books in this series take all the classics that they love and make them age appropriate for a younger audience—while still keeping the integrity and style of the original.

We hope you and you children enjoy them. We love feedback, so if you have a question or comment, stop by our website!
www.kidlito.com

[1]

INTRODUCTION

Maybe you have heard the name "Steve Jobs" before. After all, he is a hugely famous inventor. Steve Jobs worked with computers, cell phones, and many other pieces of modern technology. Without Steve Jobs, our world would not be quite the same. Maybe you have heard of "iTunes" or "iPods," and maybe you even have one. iPods and iPhones are made by Apple, which was led by Steve Jobs for a long time. Steve Jobs changed the way that we work with cell phones and computers.

He led an extraordinary life, and he always wanted to make life easier. He built an empire based on technology, and millions of people around the world use the phones that his business made. Many people say that Steve Jobs was quite a quirky man. Sometimes, the oddest people end up being the smartest people. After Steve Jobs died, the world mourned the loss of one of our greatest inventors and innovators. The life of Steve Jobs is impressive, unusual, and inspiring.

[2]
EARLY CHILDHOOD

Many people do not know that Steve Jobs was adopted. He was born in 1955, on the 24th of February, but his parents were not quite sure what to do. His mother, Joanne Schieble, had just graduated college from the University of Wisconsin, a extremely prestigious and popular school. While she was taking her classes, she began dating one of the teaching assistants, who are students that help out the professors. The teacher's assistant was named Abdulfattah Jandali. Abdulfattah was from Syria, which is a small country in the Middle East.

After Joanne and Abdulfattah graduated from the University of Wisconsin, they took a vacation to Syria. During their vacation, Joanne became pregnant, something she did not expect. This was complicated because Joanne and Abdulfattah were not married yet. They were only twenty-three years old, and they did not have enough money to raise a child on their own.

Joanne talked with a doctor, and she said that she wanted to put the baby up for adoption. Sometimes, parents are unable to take care of children, but they want their children to have good parents. Joanne told her doctor that she wanted the adoptive parents to be college graduates because college graduates are more likely to be successful.

The doctor found a couple that was interested in adopting a baby. The couple seemed nice. Both of them had graduated from college, and the husband was an exceptionally good lawyer. However, they wanted a baby girl. Eventually, the doctor found a couple to adopt Joanne's baby, but it wasn't exactly what Joanne had in mind.

The new couple had never made it past high school or college, but they were still extremely nice and loving. Their names were Paul and Clara Jobs. They took excellent care of Joanne's child, whom they had named Steve.

Paul and Clara Jobs lived in California, in a lovely place called Mountain View. Mountain View is now called Silicon Valley, a tremendously popular place in California. It wasn't called

Mountain View for nothing, though! The area is gorgeous. Around all of the beautiful scenery and all of the green grass, companies were flocking to the area. It was soon to become a spot for a lot of businesses that wanted to work with electronic things. Silicon Valley sits between San Francisco and Los Angeles, so it's a popular tourist destination! If you ever travel to California, you'll have to stop by Silicon Valley to see Steve Jobs's childhood home!

When Steve turned two years old, Paul and Clara Jobs decided that they would really like another child, so they decided to adopt again. They adopted a girl named Patty. Steve loved having a sister around!

Paul Jobs was particularly interested in fixing cars and doing mechanic work. He would work on cars in his garage, and he wanted Steve to enjoy cars just as much as he did. Paul said that Steve could work in part of the garage. Steve even had his own workbench! Steve was five years old when he started working with his father. Even from the time he was a child, Steve was raised to think and work. Working cars is difficult because everything in a car has a different purpose, and there are many small parts. Computers and cell phones are similar.

Paul was a builder, and it may have been his skill and talent that inspired Steve from such an early age. It can't be a coincidence that Steve worked so hard with his father, and then grew to be one of the greatest inventors in the world!

Cars are electrical machines. While they run on gasoline, a lot of the parts are electrical and need a battery to work. Cars were actually Steve's first experience in working with electronics. His father told him that he must always do a good job, no matter what.

In Mountain View, California, Steve loved the designs of the houses there. They had been designed by a man named Joseph Eichler. Joseph Eichler was a tremendously popular designer, and he had worked on several thousand houses in California. Many of Eichler's houses had glass walls that stretched from the ceiling to the floor, and also many sliding glass doors. Steve liked the way they looked because they were neat and classy. Steve once admitted that the houses inspired his computers later in life.

When Steve was only thirteen years old, he was working on a kit. This kit was made by Hewlett-Packard, which is a large company located near his home. Hewlett-Packard, also known as HP, is a company that manufactures electronics. Steve was terribly upset to find that his kit was missing a piece. As a result, he found the phone number of Bill Hewlett, who was a founder of HP. When Steve called, he only wanted to tell Mr. Hewlett about the missing part. But Steve got more than just a replacement part.

Mr. Hewlett was so impressed with Steve and his intelligence that he asked Steve if he wanted a summer job working at HP. In addition to that, Steve was given a package of machine parts. Steve immediately said yes and got the job. Steve also became a member of the Explorer Club at Hewlett-Packard. The club gave lessons and had meetings for children who were fascinated by electronics and mechanics. It was at one of these lessons that Steve first saw a computer.

Steve loved his classes in high school, and he also liked hanging out with his friends. His friends shared his love for electronics. Steve was also part of the computer club. There, he met someone named Steve Wozniak. His nickname was "Woz." Woz was attending a college in the area. He liked to build computers for fun. The two of them had a lot in common.

[3]

EDUCATION

Steve Jobs was extremely intelligent as a child. He knew he was smart, and so did his parents. Clara made sure he knew how to read before he even entered kindergarten. Most of the time, he was just bored in class. While all of the other kids were learning their alphabet, Steve already knew everything the teacher put on the board.

Steve went to an elementary school called Monta Loma Elementary School, and he did not like it there very much. He was a prankster as a child. Steve was often sent home by the school, but his parents were not particularly upset. Steve told his parents that he was bored and that he did not like memorizing boring things. Steve wasn't lazy though. He was simply too smart for his classes.

Steve loved his fourth grade teacher, though. Her name was Mrs. Hill and she was different from the other teachers. She knew that Steve was smarter than most kids, and she also knew that he would be bored. One time, she paid him five dollars to do all the problems in the math book. Steve thought this was odd. Mrs. Hill motivated him, and from then on Steve did not ask for payment. He would do extra work and extra math problems just for fun.

When Steve finally moved on to middle school, he was scared. Many of the kids at Crittenden Middle School were mean and cruel. They would beat up kids and wrestle in the bathrooms. Even Steve was bullied, and he wanted to change to a different school. He asked his parents if he could transfer, but it was hard for them. Paul and Clara did not have a lot of money, and they did not know if they could afford to send Steve to another school.

Steve was upset, so he told his parents that he would just quit school. His parents were intensely afraid of this since they knew how incredibly smart Steve was. Instead of just switching Steve to another school, Paul, Clara, Steve, and Patty all moved to another house that was three miles away.

Steve liked his new school very much. It was nice and clean, and there were no bullies to tease him or beat him up. Eventually, he moved onto high school. He went to a place called Homestead High School, and he liked it there. It was fifteen blocks away from his house, and he was happy to walk there each day.

The high school days were great for Steve. He pulled off a lot of pranks, like putting up flyers for Bring Your Pet to School Day and installing microphones all across his house. It was also around this time that Steve joined the Hewlett-Packard Explorer Club. Steve loved seeing the computers and all of the cool electronic technology the club showed him.

When Steve got that awesome job at Hewlett-Packard, he had a good time. He was only in high school when he worked there, and many of the workers did not like that a teenager had gotten a job simply by calling. Steve worked in an assembly line, which is when workers stand in a line, and each of them works on a separate part of a product. For example, cars are made in assembly lines. The first employee will work on one thing, and send the car down the line. The second employee works on something else. This will repeat until the car has been built.

Steve did not have such a great time in the assembly line, but he loved hanging out with all of the engineers that worked upstairs. He would have coffee and donuts with them and talk with them. He liked that much more than the assembly line.

Meanwhile, in the classroom, Steve was loving life. He liked listening to music, and he truly loved reading books. Steve had no problem reading all of the books for his English class, and enjoying them too!

When Steve reached his senior year of high school, he started dating Chrisann Brennan. They had been working on a movie project together, but they decided they truly liked each other too. Brennan liked that Steve was quirky, odd, and intelligent.

When Steve finally graduated from Homestead High School, he was not exactly sure what he wanted to do with his life. His parents wanted him to go to college, so he could get a higher education and get a good job. Steve, though, was not even sure what he wanted to do for a living. He wanted to do something adventurous and stimulating, unlike his most recent job. In order to make money, Steve, his friend Woz, and his girlfriend Chrisann were dressing up in big suits as characters from Alice in Wonderland. The pay was not great, and Steve did not enjoy it.

When Steve was searching for colleges, he found Reed College. Reed College is in Portland, Oregon, and it costs a lot of money to go there. Steve applied, and he was immediately accepted. His parents, however, were not terribly excited about him going there. After all, Reed College was expensive. Steve would not be able to afford it, and neither would Paul or Clara. They only wanted what was best for their son, and they did not think such an expensive college would help him at all.

But still, Steve wanted to go there. He wanted to learn more and experience college life. Secretly, he knew his parents were right. There was no way any of them could pay for such an expensive college.

At first, Steve attended the school and his parents paid the bills. But he was getting worried because he felt guilty about his parents paying so much money. Also, he did not like the fact that the school forced him to take certain classes, even though all colleges have required classes. Steve would often complain to Woz, who came to visit him sometimes. So, Steve did something highly unusual: he asked the dean of the college if he could attend classes for free. The dean said that Steve would not be able to graduate or get a degree, but he liked Steve's intelligence, bravery, and eagerness to learn. The dean said yes!

But because Steve wasn't actually a student of the school now, he did not have a room. Steve slept on the floor in his friends' dorm rooms, which was extremely uncomfortable. However, he did like his class. Steve loved studying eastern religions. One exceedingly popular eastern religion is Buddhism. He also liked his calligraphy classes. Calligraphy is the art of nice handwriting. Steve did not have to take any required classes now; he was allowed to study whatever he wanted for free.

If Steve Jobs had been quirky before college, he was even more odd now. Firstly, many people found his eating habits strange. Steve only wanted to eat fruits, since he had heard that only eating fruit made you seriously clean and healthy. He also this meant he could stop showering and taking baths, so he tended to carry a weird smell. Steve also did not like shoes. He preferred to walk around without socks and shoes. Even when it snowed, he only wore sandals. He must have been cold!

[4]

EARLY CAREER

After spending eighteen months at Reed College, Steve decided he wanted to drop out. He wanted to explore the world—he really wanted to travel to India! But he had had no money for college, and now he had no money to go to India. So, what did he do? He got a job at Atari!

Maybe you have played Atari games before. The Atari is a game console that was invented many years before the Playstation, Xbox, or the Wii. Many of Atari's most popular games include Pac-Man, Space Invaders, and Pong. Many Atari games are remarkably simple, and to play the games you only need a joystick and a button. While Atari games may seem tedious and easy now, they were popular when they were first invented. Atari led to the creation of modern video game consoles.

Steve knew that he needed a good job if he wanted to raise enough money to travel to India. He also knew that Atari was becoming a famous company, so it would be an excellent place to work. Steve strolled through the front doors of the company building, his flip-flops flapping on the ground. He told the service desk that he would not leave the building until he had been given a proper job.

Steve met with the chief engineer of the company and was hired instantly for his intelligence and energy towards electronics. While Steve liked the job, many people that worked there thought Steve was odd. After all, he smelled bad and did not like to wear proper shoes.

While at Atari, Steve Jobs helped make the games look much more fun. Steve enjoyed talking with his boss because they were both intelligent and they liked discussing cool ideas.

Finally, Steve had raised enough money for his vacation to India. He had a great time in the country, and he spent a lot of time studying different religions and ideas there. When he returned to the United States, Steve decided to go back to work for Atari since he liked it so much.

His boss asked him to work on a game called Pong. The game is like tennis, where two players move the joystick and bounce the ball back and forth. You score a point when your opponent misses the ball. Steve's boss wanted him to work on different versions of the game, and he also wanted Steve's friend Woz to help work on the project.

[5]

WORK AT APPLE

Steve Jobs and Steve "Woz" Wozniak were both hugely smart people and good friends. They decided that they wanted to open their own company. They were interested in computers. In the middle of the 1970s, no one had laptops or personal computers at their houses. In fact, computers back then were enormous. Woz had been trying to find a way to make computers smaller, by creating smaller circuit boards. Circuit boards are small electrical parts that help control the computers.

Steve and Woz left Atari to go start their own company. They knew they wanted to work with computers, especially since Woz was constantly inventing and making progress in the field of computer science. But, like most companies, they had to start out small. Many people do not know that Apple Computers did not have a big building at first—Steve and Woz worked in the garage in Steve's parents' house. The two of them wanted to sell circuit boards, but this idea would not actually work.

Steve and Woz thought that they could sell circuit boards, and then people would buy them to build their own computers. But computers were new at this time, and many people did not know how to build them. Even now, building a computer from scratch can be difficult. So, when they tried to sell circuit boards, the owner of a store told them they would be better off selling entire computers instead.

So, Steve and Woz borrowed computer parts from stores. They took the parts and built computers, and then sold them for money. Eventually, Steve and Woz earned a lot for their innovation and creativity. Now that they had their business rolling, they needed a name.

Since Steve ate a lot of fruit, and he really liked apples, he thought of the perfect name for his business: Apple Computers. He thought it was simple and that it sounded nice. It was also different, especially from Hewlett-Packard, which was named after its founders. Imagine if Apple had actually been named Jobs-Wozniak! People also thought the name was fascinating because no one had ever associated apples and computers together. To this day, Apple is an impressive company that is changing the way we work with phones and computers.

Woz had been working at HP at the time, and no one could have guessed the HP and Apple would become business rivals. While Woz could not work full-time with Steve Jobs, he did like helping out. Soon, he became much more involved in Apple Computers.

The first computer that Apple came out with was called the Apple I. But it was not highly advanced. A computer needs a lot of things to work. The computer is what controls every-thing, while the monitor (or the screen) shows you things. You need the keyboard to type and the mouse to move around. But the Apple I did not even have a screen or a keyboard. Steve and Woz knew that they needed to do better if they wanted to have a successful company.

So, Steve and Woz started working on the Apple II. It was going to be bigger and better, with tons of groovy features that would change the world. The Apple II had many cool features. Firstly, the screen showed things in color, which was new for the world of computers. It would also produce sound and have speakers, for cool games and other things.

Around this time, there were small, flat squares called floppy disks. These came before CDs, and people could put information on them. People put documents and other important computer stuff on them. Now, to store information, people use CDs (compact discs) and USB sticks.

Steve knew that computers had to look good, which is why many Apple products look futuristic and stylish. Sometimes, the way a thing looks is a big reason why a person buys something. So, Steve wanted to make these new computers out of plastic. Before this, computers had been made out of metal, but metal was expensive and it did not look good.

While Woz made sure the computers worked okay, Steve tried to make the computers look as good as possible. The computers needed to be neat, clean, and easy-to-use. Apple Computers was instantly successful. Companies around America started to copy Apple's design and hardware, since it was so efficient.

In just two years, Apple Computers had grown incredibly. Steve suddenly found himself one of the leaders of a growing company. He was hiring employees to work for him and build computers. He needed people to sell his computers, get parts, put the computers together, and make sure each computer worked okay. He needed to build thousands of computers.

But Steve was not such a great leader sometimes. In fact, he had a bad temper and little patience with the people that worked for him. Steve Jobs was a perfectionist, which means that he needed everything to be perfect. This was the way that his father had raised him, from the first day that Steve started working on cars in his father's garage. Steve yelled at his employees a lot. He was known for making them cry, and he even cried himself when things didn't go according to plan.

Apple had only been started in the year 1976—but just three years later, thousands of people were working for Steve Jobs. He was the face of new computers and electronic innovation. He was a creative man who always had new ideas. If there was a man that would change computers, it was Steve Jobs. People hailed him as one of the world's greatest businessmen. Steve knew exactly what to do, and he found himself making millions of dollars when he was only twenty-five.

Suddenly, Apple took a hit. Woz was riding in his private plane, when it unexpectedly crashed. It was a miracle that Woz survived. After the plane crash, he decided he did want to work for Apple. The friendship that he and Steve Jobs shared slowly drifted apart. Steve tried to get Woz to stay at Apple and continue working on computers, but Woz wanted to do other things. Steve knew that he couldn't be angry at Woz, since Woz the reason Apple had had so much success. Steve and Woz always stayed in touch with each other, though.

After Woz left, Apple wasn't the same for a while. The computers were getting really expensive, and Steve didn't like that. He wanted all of his computers to be affordable and high quality. So, he decided that it was time for a whole new type of computer, one that would change the world again.

The new computer was called the Macintosh. It was named after Macintosh apples. To this day, millions of people around the world use Macintosh computers, although they are now typically called Macs. The more recent MacBook Pro is a descendant of the first Macintosh computer. Steve knew that he needed the Macintosh to be the best computer in the world. . . but how was he going to do it?

With Woz now gone, Steve wanted a new partner. He wanted someone who was smart and creative, good with computers, and good at business. Steve set his eyes on John Sculley, who was the head of Pepsi. Pepsi is a soda; so many people didn't expect that the head of a soda company would do well in the computer business! John Sculley agreed to work with Steve Jobs because he found Steve to be an unusually interesting man. And after all, computers were getting popular with each day. Everyone knew that computers were a thing of the future, and the future was here.

The Macintosh was the start of modern computers. While the Apple I and Apple II were a bit difficult to use, the Macintosh was simple. You didn't have to be smart with computers to use it! And, for writing documents, Steve included a variety of cool fonts. Just like in his days at Reed College, Steve Jobs loved calligraphy, the art of nice handwriting. Steve wanted the computers to be accessible to all people, and he also wanted people to have fun on them.

But things did not really go as Steve had expected. Of course, it was popular for a little while. But some people did not want home computers. Others couldn't afford the Macintosh. And other customers were already dedicated to other companies. Once Apple entered the business world, it had many rivals. Other companies knew that computers were becoming popular, so engineers worked around the clock to create the best computer. At the same time that the Macintosh came out, other companies like Hewlett-Packard, Microsoft, and International Business Machines (IBM) were making computers, as well.

Steve also found himself getting into arguments with John Sculley. Sculley saw the way that people were responding to the Macintosh, and he thought that he knew how to improve things. Sculley said that Apple would not have any success making their own computers, and instead that they should make computers for other companies. Sculley thought Apple would make even more millions from this idea.

Steve Jobs, though, thought this was a horrible idea. He was immensely proud of the Macintosh and all of the work that he had been doing for years. He had spent his whole life building up to his multi-million dollar company. There was no way he would give in and start working for other businesses. He would make Apple popular, no matter what it took.

Apple had a board of businessmen that looked at the issues. The board is allowed to make decisions for the company, since they are people that do not work for the company, but can see how the company is working. Steve

Jobs approached the board and said that one of Apple's biggest problems was John Sculley. The board, however, had a different idea in mind. They decided that Steve Jobs was not fit to run the Macintosh computer project.

Steve was devastated and upset. He had been the head of all innovation at Apple, and he had just been removed. He hated not working on the Macintosh and not being in charge. Furious at the board and at all of his other workers, Steve decided it was time that he leave the Apple company. He said his goodbyes and took off, searching for new projects.

[6]

WORK AT NEXT

After leaving Apple, Steve was wondering what he would do next. He knew that the computer business was right for him. He had plenty of fresh ideas. He was smart, creative, and dedicated to making computers the best they could be. And he even saw the world changing around him. Computers were not only a thing for businessmen and technologically apt people. Everyone was beginning to use computers now: people at home, students at school, and even children. A whole generation was growing up with a mouse and keyboard at their fingertips.

Steve also wanted to get back at Apple for treating him poorly. So, he started another company, one that he called NeXT. He wanted everyone to be able to use these new computers, although he thought that students and teachers would have the best use for them. Computers were changing classrooms across the world, and they would continue to do so for decades to come.

But starting a company is extraordinarily difficult. It costs a lot of money and, even though Steve had millions of dollars, it was difficult. Each computer was too expensive, and schools could not afford expensive computers. When Steve first revealed the first NeXT computer, he was extremely nervous. He stood on a stage, in front of tons of people, describing the NeXT computer and explaining why it was the best.

Steve knew that the price of the computer, $6,500, would disappoint everyone. It was simply too expensive. Of course, computers were modern and important, but many people just could not spend all of that money on a computer. Especially students, who were already paying thousands of dollars to go to college, could not find the money for that. Steve tried to play with the audience's mind. He listed all of the NeXT computer's features, making each one sound hugely expensive and important. At the end, he said that it would only cost $6,500, hoping people would not think that was too bad.

People did not like the sound of it, though. What made it even worse was that the NeXT computer would not even come out for two years. So people had to pay all of this money and wait for it to come out? NeXT was not going too well for Steve so far. At the end of the meeting, a violinist that Steve had hired walked onto the stage. While the NeXT computer played music, the violinist played music, as well. And there, on that stage, a human and a computer played a duet together—this was unprecedented and unheard of. It was a terrific way to end the meeting, because everyone cheered and was amazed.

Many people looked to Microsoft for an opinion on the NeXT computer. Now, Microsoft obviously would not have anything good to say about it because Microsoft and NeXT were rivals. The leader of Microsoft was Bill Gates, an inventor who is just as great and amazing as Steve Jobs. For a very long time, Microsoft was much more popular than Apple. Bill Gates said that the NeXT computer was disappointing since it did not offer anything important. It was just the Macintosh computer, with some cool and fun features.

Needless to say, NeXT did not last too long. It was a complete failure, and Steve Jobs had spent millions upon millions of dollars to keep it alive. In the end, however, the company crashed and Steve was sent looking for a new job.

Several important things happened in Steve's live during the time he spent leading NeXT. For one, he was immensely curious about his birth parents. When he was a kid, Paul and Clara had always been extraordinarily open about the fact that Steve was adopted. He had always wanted to know about his real mother and his real father.

Steve looked at his birth certificate, something that is created for every child that is born. Birth certificates list the name of the baby, the mother, the father, and the doctor that delivered the baby. Steve found the name of the doctor, and then he found the doctor at the hospital. The doctor told Steve about his mother.

Joanna Schieble, Steve's mother, had not been married to Abdulfattah Jandali for long. The two of them had gotten a divorce soon after Steve was born, and Joanne Jandali became Joanna Schieble again. Steve found out that Joanne had a daughter! Her name was Mona, and Steve quickly arranged a meeting together. Joanna and Mona, who was a published, were supremely happy to meet each other and speak.

As for Abdulfattah Jandali, there was a mighty strange coincidence. Steve and Jandali had both lived in the same city. Jandali ran a restaurant in Silicon Valley—a restaurant that Steve had visited frequently. Even stranger, Steve and his father had met before, but neither knew that they were related to each other. Before Jandali knew that Steve Jobs was his son, Steve was already becoming famous. He used to tell people that the founder of Apple Computers would come into his restaurant all the time. It was Mona that told Jandali the truth—that Steve was actually his son!

A long time ago, Steve had had a daughter with his girlfriend Chrisann Brennan, even though the two were never married. Steve broke up with Chrisann, and he did not want to take care of his daughter, who had been named Lisa. Even though Mona told Steve that he should spend more time with Lisa, Steve wanted another girlfriend. He was over thirty years old, and he wanted to get married.

Steve had had many girlfriends, but none of them seemed particularly special. That is, until Steve met his future wife in 1990. Her name is Laurene Powell, and she was a graduate student at the time. She and Steve had a lot in common: both of them were very intelligent, and they were both vegetarians. Vegetarians are people that do not eat any meat—and Steve's odd diet definitely qualified him for that!

For a year, Steve and Laurene dated, until they decided that both of them really wanted to get married. Steve and Laurene got married at Yosemite National Park, a truly beautiful park in northern California. Soon after they were married, Laurene gave birth to a son. They named him Reed Paul Jobs. Steve thought it would be a good idea to name his son after Reed College, the school he had attended years ago. His son's middle name, Paul, was also Steve's father's name.

Two years after Reed Jobs was born, a tragedy hit the Jobs family. Paul Jobs died, and Steve was devastated. This made Steve rethink his life. As he remembered all of the great times he and his father had spent together, fixing cars and making everything perfect, Steve realized that he needed to be there for his daughter Lisa. By now, Lisa was already a teenager. Steve actually wanted to spend more time with her, so that she would be able to know her father.

[7]

WORK AT PIXAR

More companies were on the rise during this time—but not all of them focused on computers. George Lucas was a rising star. His company, Lucasfilm, had just produced three Star Wars movies: A New Hope, The Empire Strikes Back, and The Return of the Jedi. The world loved the Star Wars movies, and George Lucas was now swimming in money.

Steve was tremendously interested in working with George Lucas, especially because he was such a fan of the Star Wars movies. Steve liked George Lucas because he was creative and smart, and his movies changed the science-fiction genre forever. To this day, the Star Wars universe is growing, with new video games, toys, and even a new movie trilogy coming soon. It's no wonder that Steve loved Lucas's work!

George was happy to work with Steve. In fact, George Lucas was interested in expanding his company into computer animation. Computer animation is responsible for any cartoons or animated movies. Steve took on the job with excitement and interest. He wanted the company to be named Pixar, which is now one of the most popular movie-making companies in the world.

During the time that Steve worked at Pixar, the company started losing money. Steve had worked on new ways to animate movies, but no one wanted to buy the programs he created. Mainly, like many of his previous products, they did not sell because they were just too expensive. But Pixar did not need to worry because Steve willingly used over fifty million dollars to help Pixar get through the tough times.

Steve started selling computers at Pixar—computers that made animation. He found computer animation particularly interesting, and he thought that selling computers would help Pixar raise money. He wanted to make computer animation simple and easy to use, but also more advanced than the programs that already existed. Steve met many people at Pixar, including a man named John Lasseter. Steve and John both wanted the best for Pixar, and they wanted to do new and surprising things with animation. Their bosses, however, were highly restrictive.

A team of designers, with Steve Jobs and John Lasseter, worked on a short animated film that was tremendously successful. It was called Luxo Jr. It was entered into a competition, but it did not win any awards. It showed Steve, though, that there may be a new day to express his creativity and make Pixar famous.

As he struggled onwards, Pixar started to lose money. The animated short movies were not extremely popular at first, and many of the heads of the company were arguing furiously with each other. Everyone had a different idea about what would make Pixar money. Steve decided that Pixar needed totally new workers. He began firing the people that were hurting Pixar's business, determined that cleaning out the employees would help.

People started to love the computers and programs that Pixar was designing. Pixar sold machines called Pixar Image Computers. These computers, along with programs such as Pixar's Showplace, were built so that normal, everyday people could animate short movies. Steve wanted everyone in the world to share his excitement, so he needed to make them accessible.

John Lasseter came to Steve one day with an idea. He said that he wanted to make a new animated short film, about a toy. The only problem was that they were very short on money, and they did not know if they would be able to afford making the film. Steve took a look at the outline for John's idea, and he thought it was amazing. He gladly used $300,000 of his own money to help out the project.

The short movie, which was called Tin Toy, won an award and gave everyone at Pixar new hope. Perhaps the company would not fail after all!

The Walt Disney Company, one of the most successful business in the world, has been around for decades. It saw the work that Pixar was doing, and it admired John Lasseter. The heads of Disney asked John Lasseter to work with them, since they wanted to work on a new movie. John Lasseter, though, was committed to Pixar and working with Steve Jobs. There was no way he'd be leaving.

Steve Jobs really wanted to work with Disney, though. He knew that Disney was one of the richest companies in the world, and they had some of the smartest designers. Also, Steve loved Walt Disney, who had showed the world that imagination and creativity are great things. Steve went to the Disney Company and asked them for money, so that he could create three new projects. He told Pixar that the three projects would be normal movies, not short films. Steve wanted the movies to be computer animated. A project like this would definitely change the way that movies work.

The folks at Disney agreed because they thought that Steve was smart and eager enough to get the job done.

Steve talked with John Lasseter and a team of designers about the job. John Lasseter said that he had the perfect idea in mind—a story about toys that are actually alive. They knew that kids would love the movie, because the idea was cool and unique. They also knew that adults would love the movie for its humor, its plot, and the memories they had of playing with toys.

If you have seen Toy Story, you know that Woody and Buzz are two very different characters, and they argue a lot during the movie. This is because the heads of Disney and Pixar knew that there had to be conflict. If Woody and Buzz were friends the entire movie, it would not be very interesting.

Steve, the designers, and many others held several meetings about Toy Story, and it seemed that the story was changing every time they talked about it. One of the men that worked at Disney, a man called Katzenberg, tried to control the entire project. He told the designers exactly how the movie plot should go, and because of this the first draft of Toy Story did not go so well.

When people told Katzenberg that he should give the Pixar workers complete control over the movie story, he agreed. Steve Jobs knew that now, Pixar could work on Toy Story the way they wanted to. Katzenberg and the Disney executives would not be interfering anymore.

Steve really wanted to make the movie perfect—after all, he was a perfectionist. He would watch each scene over and over again, and tell the designers exactly what would make it better. There were dozens of edits and revisions and changes, so that many of the workers were sick and tired of the movie. But Steve continued. He would not stop until Toy Story was the best it could be.

Obviously, Toy Story is one of the most successful movies of all time. The very first weekend it opened in theaters; the movie raised thirty million dollars. Some websites even re-gard it with perfect ratings. Magazines and newspapers hailed Toy Story as inventive, crea-tive, and beautiful. It was truly a movie that would change the world of computer anima-tion.

Steve and the rest of Pixar celebrated Toy Story's success. He had created a deal with Disney that said he would create three movies. Now that the first was done, there were still two more movies to make. Disney was chang-ing too, and many of the top executives were going to other companies. The deal was com-pleted, although Steve Jobs was not very in-volved in those projects.

Toy Story was Pixar's monster hit. Pixar went on to great more than a dozen top movies in a row. People were amazed with the brilliant sto-ries, with the quality of the animation, and with the new and incredible movie experience. Pixar was growing, and it continues to make movies today. Its most popular movie is Toy Story 3, which came out in 2010.

But Steve Jobs's time at Pixar was about to come to an end. While NeXT had collapsed completely by this point, his older company, Apple, was going through many changes. And

Steve thought that he just might be able to help them out.

[8]

RETURN TO APPLE

While Steve had been trying to revive the struggling NeXT company, and also while he had been working with computers and animation at Pixar, Apple Computers had not been doing so well. The people who were running Apple simply did not have the imagination and creativity that Steve had. They only cared about making money, and not about making high-quality products. Steve knew that this needed to change.

He wanted to return—but he wanted to be the CEO. CEO stands for Chief Executive Officer, and this is the person that runs an entire business. He told friends that he did not want to barge through the doors of the Apple headquarters and demand that they make him the CEO. He wanted to talk with people at the company, and uses his words and his wit to get back into the business.

The CEO of Apple Computers was a man named Gil Amelio. He had taken control after a few of the other CEOs had been removed for not running the company right. Steve wanted to meet with Amelio and discuss Apple.

Steve told him that everyone knew Apple was going downhill. The company was losing a lot of money, and there seemed to be no solution. Steve said that he was the only person that could save the company. Apple needed new computer products, new ones that would change the world like never before. But Amelio was skeptical. He did not have any creative visions for the future. He did not know if anything would be able to replace the Macintosh computer.

Steve Jobs knew one thing: something had to replace the Macintosh computer. Other companies were racing ahead of Apple, and their products were much cheaper. Apple's technology was slow and behind the times. If Apple did not come out with something new, the company would fall apart.

The board of businessmen that controlled Apple wanted Steve Jobs back. Everyone knew that something needed to be done. They all looked to Steve to help them get Apple back on its feet. Steve was the man with the plan: with his innovation and his creativity, perhaps he could save the company.

But Steve was not sure he really wanted to return to Apple. When he had last worked there, years ago, people had treated him terribly poorly. He had been taken down as the CEO last time, and he did not want that to happen again. And in addition to all of that, he and his wife Laurene were welcoming a new baby into the family. They now had two children: Reed Paul Jobs and Erin Sienna Jobs. Could he handle being the CEO of one of the world's biggest companies and be the father of two children?

Steve said yes. It was a big commitment to make, and one that would change the world. He remembered creating Apple with Woz all those years ago, and he couldn't just let Apple sink into the ground. He would return there, and he would do his best to make Apple the world's best business ever.

By this point, around 1996, Steve had billions and billions of dollars in his wallet. He didn't need an annual salary – the amount of money that someone is paid each year. He wanted to use his money to bring Apple to its feet and change the world. He did not pay himself for the work he would do in the next few years.

When Steve stepped into the role of CEO, he ruled Apple with an iron fist. He had only planned to stay there for a few months, so he knew that any changes he made needed to matter. Like at Pixar, he fired a lot of Apple's employees. Steve knew that hiring too many workers cost a lot of money—money that Apple could be using. He wanted very few, very smart people working on his projects.

Steve looked at any Apple products that were doing poorly, and he told his employees to stop selling them. Apple would only sell things that the world could use. This would boost the company's reputation.

When 1997 rolled around, Steve Jobs made a deal that many people thought was odd. He wanted to become business partners with Apple's rival, Microsoft. Loyal Apple fans thought this was a terrible idea! Why would two rivals become partners?

Well, Steve admired Bill Gates, who was the CEO of Microsoft. Steve and Bill were both majorly smart people, whose computers were selling worldwide. Microsoft had efficient Internet browsers. Some modern Internet browsers include Internet Explorer, Google Chrome,

Mozilla Firefox, and Safari. Steve Jobs wanted to use Microsoft's Internet browsers. While many people did not like this idea, it made Apple's profits soar. Everyone liked Apple computers, and they were made even better with Microsoft's Internet browser.

But there was something else that Steve needed to figure out. He needed to come out with something new: a new computer that would astound the world. The iMac was the new big thing. The term "iMac" stood for Internet Macintosh, and this was the beginning of Apple's "i" products, such as the iPhone, iPod, and iPad. The iMac was made for people who wanted to use the Internet, and the 1990s was the rise of the Internet. Websites were being made by the minute, and Steve Jobs knew that the Internet was a thing of the future. If he wanted Apple to make a lot of money, it would need to be able to have products that used the Internet well.

The world loved the iMac. Steve Jobs's return to Apple had been an enormous success, and it truly was his intelligence that saved the company. Around the world, everyone wanted an iMac. The personal computer became so popular that it was sold more than any other computer by any other company.

After the success of the iMac, Steve Jobs knew that there was no way he could leave Apple. He had only planned to stay for a few months, but too many great things were happening. He was immensely happy with what Apple was doing. Steve would make computers for a whole new generation of kids.

Apple grew at an alarming rate. Millions of people wanted iMacs and other Apple products. Steve knew that it was finally time to open stores, so that people could walk through a set of doors, browse Apple products, talk with friendly employees, and get all the information they could. But Steve also knew that Apple stores could not look like any store that you might see. He wanted to build them out of glass so that they would look cool and futuristic. People around the world would flock to the glass Apple stores.

Even now, you can do much more than just buy things in the Apple store. There are employees there that will help you with any problems you have. If your computer is broken, you can bring it in, and the employees will take a look at it. You can also do this with iPods or any other products that Apple invented. Also, if you do not know how to use computers, the employees will take you step-by-step through the set-up and help you learn.

As the 1990s came to a close, Steve realized that his predictions had come true. He always knew that computers would become extremely popular. People use computers every single day. At work, in the classroom, and at home, people can use computers for fun and while they work.

But did Steve Jobs stop at the iMac and the Apple stores? Of course not! There was more work to be done. Steve looked at CDs, and he wanted to change the way that people listened to music. Already, people were using a product called the Walkman. The Walkman was a small disc-like machine that was the size of a CD. A person could put the CD into the Walkman, connect some headphones, and listen to music. But Steve wondered: what if people didn't need CDs anymore?

Steve found out a way to change music forever. Now, people could take their favorite CD and put it into the computer. The computer would scan the contents of the CD and put it onto the computer. Now, people could use their computers to listen to music! The Apple program was called iTunes, and iTunes still makes tons of money today. Now, you can buy almost any song by any artist. Most songs only cost ninety-nine cents, and you are allowed to keep it forever.

But there was one problem with this: What if you bought songs on a CD, but did not want to use a Walkman? People wanted to walk around and listen to music, but not carry a CD-sized Walkman around with them. Business and companies quickly adapted to the change in the music industry. New, tiny machines came out—ones that you could just slip into your pocket. They are called MP3 players, since MP3 is the name of a music file on a computer.

People could download music from their computers onto the MP3 players, and this made people truly happy. No CDs needed! Music was now more portable than ever.

So now that Steve Jobs had changed the way that humans listen to and travel with music, it was time for Apple to come out with their own MP3 player. But Steve knew that it needed to better than MP3 players made by other companies. Once again, Steve would not fail to disappoint.

The first iPod came out in 2001. It was Apple's first portable music-listening device, and iPods are still popular today. Steve made it so that people using Apple computers and Microsoft computers could attach their iPods and download music, so that more people would be able to buy and use them. This was a brilliant move on the part of Steve Jobs, because was not limiting his customers to Apple fans only.

But there was a now a pretty big problem. Music companies were losing tons of money. People were borrowing each other's CDs and sharing music. One person could buy a CD and lend it to five of his friends. Instead of five people buying one CD each, they would share the CD. Music companies were upset. The revolution in the music industry was hurting their business.

Of course, though, Steve Jobs had a fantastic idea. What if people could buy music online? What if, with the click of a button, you could see your favorite songs in your iTunes library? He wanted to open an online music store, where people could search their favorite songs and purchase them for ninety-nine cents each. This way, people would share CDs less.

The idea worked. Billions and billions of songs have been bought on iTunes. Steve Jobs changed the way we use computers, the way we travel with portable music, and the way we even purchase music. Technology was changing before the world's eyes every single day, but there was no way Steve could stop there. There was still plenty of more work to do.

Steve said that this was one of the happiest times in his life. He was in control of Apple, which was swimming in money. He was still in control of Pixar, whose movies were being shown around the world and winning tons of awards. And on top of all of that, his family life was going very well. His daughter with Chrisann Brennan, Lisa, was a successful college student. She had graduated from Harvard after studying journalism and writing. As for his three children with his wife Laurene, he was happy. With Laurene, he had two daughters, Erin and Eve, and his son Reed.

His return to Apple was successful. As Apple led the way into the twenty-first century, the company continued to show the world just how great it was. To this day, people are obsessed with Apple products. The creation of the iPod led to new versions of it. iPods have been adjusted to have bigger screens, and some of them now even have touch screens. The iPod Nano was a big hit among customers, since it was small enough to fit in a person's palm.

Apple also knew that the market for cell phones was about to skyrocket. The blueprints for the iPhone went into design, and the phone is incredibly successful. Many people like the iPhone for its ability to act as both an iPod and a phone at the same time.

Humans' lives are becoming more and more dependent on technology. The newest form of technology is called the tablets. Tablets look like big phones, although they are meant for reading, playing games, and surfing the Internet. Many companies are competing for who has the best tablet, and Apple's iPad seems to be doing very well. Many people have complained, however, that Apple's products are becoming too expensive for the common person to buy.

Even the prices of Apple's computers have recently skyrocketed. While at one point everyone wanted to own an iMac, now Apple widely sells its laptop, called the MacBook. Like the iPod, there are many different versions of the MacBook. Once thing is certain: Apple will continue to change the world.

[9]

PHILANTHROPY

When a person is tremendously wealthy, people expect that person to give away some of their money. After all, there are plenty of people in this world who are homeless and extremely hungry. There will always be people who need help. The public looks to rich people for help and to share their money with people in need. Bill Gates, the CEO of Microsoft, is one of the world's most famous philanthropists. A philanthropist is someone who helps others, either by visiting them and helping or donating money.

But many people did not know whether Steve Jobs was a philanthropist. No one could find any record of him donating any of his money to any charity or organization. Sometimes, people would criticize him for being greedy with his money—but is that actually the case?

Steve Jobs was not actually greedy. Despite the fact that he never publicly donated money, he went years without paying himself. When he returned to Apple, he was only paid one dollar per year. Of course, he could afford to be paid one dollar per year. But, unlike many millionaires, Steve did not want to keep all of his money for himself. He put much of his money into Apple, to try to make it a better company and to help the world.

Some people have heard rumors that Steve Jobs donated money anonymously—meaning that he gave money away without revealing his name. This is possible, but no one really knows for sure. It will always be a mystery.

[10]

DEATH AND LEGACY

After Steve Jobs returned to Apple, he discovered that he was sick. He found out that something was wrong with him in 2003, when he went to see the doctor. The doctors examined him and found out that he had cancer.

Cancer is a terrible disease that some people get. The disease can infect certain areas of the body, and in Steve Jobs in affected his pancreas. The pancreas is an organ inside your body. It sits near the stomach, and it helps digest food. Steve knew that he needed to do something. If he didn't, the cancer would grow, and he would only get sicker.

Steve had surgery the next year, to remove the cancer. While the cancer was gone, he was still slightly sick. He tried to change what he ate in order to help. But despite all of his efforts, he still did not feel good. The sickness made him believe more firmly in himself. He was glad that, throughout his life, he did what he wanted to do. He was hugely proud of his achievements.

Steve started to take some time off from Apple because he was feeling sick and tired. But despite the cancer, he still managed to make Apple a big success. He came out with new iPods, the iPhone, and the iPad, all while taking care of his family and dealing with the pancreatic cancer.

In the summer of 2011, Steve Jobs realized he needed to leave Apple. He was over fifty years old now, and the cancer was making him feel sicker each day. As much as he loved working at Apple and coming out with cool new technology, he really wanted to spend time with his family. He cared a lot about his wife and his children, and they mattered more to him than Apple.

A few months after Steve Jobs left Apple, he passed away. He died on October 5th, 2011. On that day, all of his family was at his house. His wife Laurene, his children, his sister Patti, and his sister Mona all wanted to spend time with him, and they were all glad that they were there in Steve's final moments.

The world was devastated over the loss of Steve Jobs. One of our greatest innovators had passed away. Steve's millions of fans were very sad, and they wanted to celebrate his life. On the glass windows of Apple stores across the country, people wrote little messages on sticky notes. People thanked him for all of the work that he did, and for changing the world and making it easier.

Steve Jobs left behind an amazing legacy. He was a master businessman, despite his quirks. His creative and intelligent mind paved the way for new technology. While Steve Jobs never actually invented computers or phones, he took old ideas and he made them new. He understood the way the world worked, and the way that people lived their lives.

People will continue to enjoy Steve's technology for decades to come. He changed the way we use computers, phones, and tablets, making everything simpler and neater. Around the world, people use MacBooks to do their homework, snap pictures with iPods, and text friends using iPhones. Steve Jobs had the vision for a better world, and he definitely accomplished his goal.

BIBLIOGRAPHY

Isaacson, Walter. Steve Jobs. New York: Simon & Schuster, 2011. Print.

Pollack, Pam, and Meg Belviso. Who Was Steve Jobs? New York: Grosset & Dunlap, 2012. Print.

Sorkin, Andrew Ross. "The Mystery of Steve Jobs's Public Giving."Dealbook.nytimes.com. New York Times, 29 Aug. 2011. Web. 06 July 2013. <http://dealbook.nytimes.com/2011/08/29/the-mystery-of-steve-jobss-public-giving/>.